By Gail Johnson

To access audio visit:
www.halleonard.com/mylibrary

Enter Code
5450-9063-2084-8776

This book is dedicated to my Mom, Aaron, Tamina, Donna, Venus, Bernita, my Dad, DeNichole, Chrissy, and...Bubu.

ISBN 978-0-7935-9870-0

7777 W. BLUEMOUND RD. P.O. BOX 13819 MILWAUKEE, WI 53213

Visit Hal Leonard Online at
www.halleonard.com

ACKNOWLEDGMENTS

ACKNOWLEDGMENTS

There are many people in my life who have assisted me in becoming the person, the professional musician, and the educator that I am today. My Uncle Bill heads the list. He served as a mentor and manager for the very first band that I performed with in Philadelphia, PA. I'd also like to thank some of the musicians in Philly that "let a girl" play in the band: Tyrone Reeves, Bob Allen, Rodger "Prophet" Lee, Nelson Mayrant, Greg Peeler, Vincent Lane, Brian Williams, Doug Grisby, Donald Robinson, and many, many others. I was welcomed in Los Angeles by my brother, Vidais Lovette, Hershel Happiness, Ricky Smith, James Manning, Norman Brown, Pam Williams, Charles Love, and Tio Banks, just to name a few. Much love to the staff at Musicians Institute: Henry "Sol-eh" Brewer (whose inspiration has been invaluable in the making of this book), Larry Steelman (for taking me on), and Rose Bradley (sistah to sistah). Lastly, I'd like to thank the entire staff at Hal Leonard Corporation, who spent many hours helping me put it all together, as well as the musicians who played on the recording, Fred Dinkins (drums) and Tony Marshall (guitar).

Contents

Introduction

This book is designed to illustrate some of the most common patterns, progressions, and licks found in funk music. Focus is placed on the keyboard player's function in the rhythm section and on various keyboard setups and instrumentation. The primary concern in funk music is the *groove*—the cyclical repetition of a musical phrase. Each time the pattern is played, an "energy" or "drive" elevates the music to a new level. Think of a circle going round and round, creating a gravitational lift—otherwise described as *rhythm.*

What Is Funk?

The term *funk* most likely evolved from the Central African Ki-Kongo word *lu'funki,* which describes the positive energy of exertion (as well as a strong body odor!). One is praised for being funky and full of integrity—for having "worked out" their artistry.

By the late 1960s, funk was established as a brand new art form, a form spiritually influenced by its roots in soul music, R&B, and jazz. James Brown's "Papa's Got a Brand New Bag" is now considered the first funk recording, though some would argue that The Isley Brothers' "Testify, Parts 1 & 2" is the original funk tune. Regardless, funk turned the beat around, placing the emphasis on the downbeat (beats 1 and 3) instead of the backbeat (beats 2 and 4) as other musical forms such as shuffle, swing, and gospel previously had done. The formula for funk rhythm consists of a variety of polyrhythms: a strong backbeat from the drummer, a syncopated bass line, counter guitar line, counter keyboard chord rhythm, heavy soul vocals, and a definite pulse on the *one!* (James Brown's famous line, "Hit me!," meant to accent the downbeat, or beat 1, of the measure.) African American music forms such as boogie woogie, New Orleans second line, blues, jazz, and gospel all maintain similar characteristics of rhythm as their most basic ingredient, but also rely heavily on a "call and response" between musicians. In funk, the interplay between musicians must lock together to create what is called the *pocket.* While the musicians lock into the pocket, the listener becomes locked into the hypnotic trance of the groove. It is common for the audience to sing the chorus with the band, as in Kool & The Gang's "Celebrate good time...come on!" Surely the groove also compels you to "Dance to the Music" (Sly & The Family Stone). It is this "togetherness" and connectedness between audience and performer that has sustained the popularity of funk.

The Keyboard Setup

Funk keyboardists have transcended mere "piano playing," taking the keyboard to a new horizon. Below is an illustration of how many funk keyboardists set up their various keyboards, including: Fender Rhodes, Arp Odyssey, Mini-moog, Hammond B3, and Honer D6 Clavinet.

Most classic funk keyboard sounds can be emulated with some well-chosen patches, or presets, on a single modern synth. Here are the essentials:

Clav (shortened for *clavinet*)—The most popular model in the seventies was the Honer D6 model. Today, many sound modules and synthesizers have this "pseudo-harpsichord" sounding instrument. Various patches using one adjective or another and the word "clav" to describe its sound (i.e. resoclav, phaseclav, clav 1, etc.) have become stock sounds in today's keyboards. Locate a couple of these patches, and use them when learning clavinet parts.

Rhodes—Formerly known as the Fender Rhodes (standard 73-key or 88-key suitcase), it is today better known as the electric piano. However, the Rhodes sound of the funk era had a thick, full sound—unlike some of the bell-timbered electric piano patches made popular through the digital dynasty. There are various Rhodes sounds available, including some with effects like tremolo and chorus.

Organ—Although many artists used various organs, including the Farfisa (more popular in the rock idiom), most preferred and lugged that 600-pound giant called the Hammond Organ. It offered several different models, but the funk masters just had to have a B3. Its full and robust sound could hum in the background and in a moment's notice screech and wail into some of the most outstanding solos and rhythm chops. Look for patches that feature a percussive edge over deep harmonic tones.

Bass Synth—The Mini-moog reigned king for a long time! Its monophonic sound gave rise to a new technique: two-handed playing using the pitch and modulation wheels, including slides (wherein your thumb or palm slides up or down the keyboard in a single strike). Find bass sounds that are more rounded, unlike those of the popping or slapping variety. Set your keyboard to mono mode (only one key can sound at a time).

Synth—Synth sounds are widely varied. Many of the instruments found on funk recordings have long been passé; however, there are various synthesizers and sound modules that try to capture some of those analog sounds. One patch to look for is "lead synth," which emulates the "worm" synth sound (usually monophonic) with either a warm, soft attack or the kind with a buzzing edge that cuts through with a high resonance. Another patch needed is of the polyphonic variety (four or more voices played at a time). This will be used to perform "pads" or chordal beds that also make use of the modulation and pitch wheels. This sound can be warm, like french horns, or bright and glaring, like trumpets. Both sounds have a strong attack value (as opposed to patches with swells). Patches that swell (gradually achieve their fullest sounds) also make use of aftertouch, which is available on newer synths. For instance, you can set your keyboard to kick in a modulation effect by simply pressing harder on the key. For now, a lead patch and a pad patch will suffice for learning many funky synth parts.

Remember: when learning a specific part (whether it be a Rhodes part or a clav part), always use the corresponding sound to achieve the best results in your study. Most of the examples in this book will be two to eight measures in length, thus easy to commit to memory.

Listen Up!

Much of funk music has not been written down. To study the music, one had to listen to recordings or learn from other players. In many four-track or eight-track recordings, the keyboard was generally deep in the mix, and trying to learn exactly what was played was a challenge. Listening to great funk artists like James Brown, Parliament, Sly & The Family Stone, and others gives you an idea of what was happening socially, politically, and musically from the late 1960s to the early 1980s. The inner city was making a statement, the underpriviledged were taking a stand, the racial divide was trying to close its gap, and funk music was the catalyst! George Clinton and his P-Funk empire sum it up well in their track "One Nation Under a Groove."

Funk was probably the last form of music to be played by trained jazz musicians, a distinction that helps solidify these musicians' place in popular culture while also assuring a high level of musical integrity within the form. Though you've probably heard many funk songs, you may not be familiar with the keyboardists who have applied their artistry to this form—artists such as Bernie Worrel of Parliament Funkadelic; Larry Dunn of Earth, Wind & Fire; Bobby Byrd of James Brown and the Famous Flames; or Booker T. Jones of Booker T. and the MG's (Memphis Group). With the advent of synthesizers and an ever-increasing move forward in keyboard technology, these players were among the readiest to find expression in these new sounds, while also exploring musical progressions in new ways. They hung onto their roots in gospel, soul, and jazz, but made the songs a joy to play by infusing them with the grooving beat of funk. Their simplistic, polyrhythmic funk style has earned them a special place in popular music, and their work is still admired by many keyboardists today.

The purpose of this book is to get you comfortable playing in the funk music style. Before you begin learning or re-acquainting yourself with funk music, take time to listen to the suggested recordings. Place yourself in the band, feel the music pulsate the groove within, and remember: put it *on the one!*

Dexter Wansell

Bobby Byrd
James Brown & The Famous

Leon Huff

Larry Dunn
Earth, Wind & Fire

Herbie Hancock

Valerie Simpson

Stevie Wonder

Herschel Happiness
Graham Central station

**Hawk Wolinsky/
Keven Murphy**
Rufus & Chaka Khan

Booker T. Jones
Booker T. & The MG's

Billy Beck
Ohio Players

Lil' Sister
Sly & The Family Stone

Bernie Worrell
Parliament/Funkadelic

Donny Hathaway

Billy Preston

Chris Jasper
Isley Bros.

Amir Bayyan
Kool & The Gang

Chester Thompson
Tower of Power

**Gregory Johnson/
Thomas Campbell**
Cameo

Patrice Rushen

Lonnie Jordan

Curtis Mayfield

ARTIST	SONG	PART
Billy Preston	Outta Space	Clav
Billy Preston	Will It Go 'Round in Circles	Piano/Organ
Stevie Wonder	Boogie on Reggae Woman	Clav/Bass Synth
Chris Jasper	It's Your Thang	Piano
Chester Thompson	What Is Hip?	Organ
Parliament	Knee Deep	Piano/Synth
Parliament	Flashlight	Bass Synth/Synth
Carl Carlton	Bad Mama Jama	Bass Synth
George Duke	Dukey Stick	Synth
Herbie Hancock	Chameleon	Clav/Rhodes
Ohio Players	Skin Tight	Rhodes
James Brown	Get Up I Feel Like Being a Sex Machine	Piano
The Time	Wild & Loose	Synth
Earth, Wind & Fire	Magic Mind	Rhodes
Sly & the Family Stone	Dance to the Music	Organ
Isley Brothers	Work to Do	Clav
Stevie Wonder	Higher Ground	Clav
War	All Day Music	Organ
The Whispers	And the Beat Goes On	Clav/Synth
Tom Browne	Funkin' for Jamaica	Piano
Rusken	Haven't You Heard	Piano
Chaka Khan & Rufus	Tell Me Something Good	Clav
Rufus	You Got the Love	Clav/Rhodes
Evelyn "Champagne" King	Shame	Rhodes
Brothers Johnson	I'll Be Good to You	Rhodes
Al Green	Love and Happiness	Organ
The Gap Band	Outstanding	Piano
The Gap Band	Burn Rubber on Me	Bass Synth
Earth, Wind & Fire	Got to Get You into My Life	Rhodes

James Brown

James Brown's music changed the rhythmic pattern of the entire rhythm section. Straight quarter notes on the hi-hat, a syncopated bass line, and counter-rhythmic guitar picking lines are all elements of his style. Patterned guitar strumming and simple horn lines in three-part harmony accenting the downbeat are also common elements of Brown's style. All this with added organ rhythms and piano solos created a new sound sensation in the late 1960s.

James's gospel roots allowed his vocal repetitions to further fuel the fire for him and his Famous Flames. The excitement and dance-stomping grooves on his recordings were raised to the highest level in his live stage performances. Musicians like Maceo & the King's Men, Fred Wesley & the JB's, The Horny Horns, and Bootsy Collins enjoyed lasting careers due to the groundwork laid by James Brown, the "Godfather of Soul." For a good introduction to James Brown's style, listen to the piano solo on "Get Up I Feel Like Being a Sex Machine."

Billy Preston

A prolific songwriter and outstanding keyboardist, Billy enjoyed success as one of the top studio session players in Los Angeles in the early 1970s. He is probably equally famous for his organ chops and rhythmic piano chording. He has a great vocal style as well, exemplified on his hit single "With You I'm Born Again." Billy Preston brought his church-rockin' keyboard style to touring groups like The Rolling Stones, Little Richard, and the Beatles, and to recording artists like Barbra Streisand, Sly & The Family Stone, and Ray Charles. His appearance on *Let It Be* and in concerts with Mahalia Jackson and Sam Cooke attest to his in-depth versatility as an instrumentalist and vocalist. Whether he is writing for film or records, playing in rock or funk bands, Billy's keyboard style is unique. To get a sense of Billy Preston's sound, listen to "Will It Go Round in Circles," and "Outta Space."

Bernie Worrell/Parliament Funkadelic

"One Nation Under a Groove" describes the philosophy of the funk music movement of the 1970s, and Bernie was in full charge of those funk keyboard parts in hits like "Mothership Connection," "Chocolate City," and "Aqua Boogie." Listen to the acoustic piano parts and you'll hear a compilation of jazz voicings and blues licks topped off with a funky rhythmic groove that is truly inspiring to listen to. Mr. Worrell has organ skills, too: listen to "Sacred Place" with Bootsy Collins. And on the bass synth, Bernie continuously pumps up the funk riffs in a pentatonic pattern that is as varied and refreshing each time the bar rolls around again, locking into the drums and not letting go. Sometimes their jams would be well over ten minutes long, and the dance crowd would be asking for more. Bernie's funk in full effect can be heard on Bootsy's Rubber Band, Brides of Funkenstein, Parliament, Funkadelic, The Horney Horns, and Parlet. For a great groove sampling, check out the song "Flash Light."

George Duke

George Duke is a multi-keyboardist extraordinaire! He has worked with many greats over the years, including Jean Luc Ponty, Frank Zappa & The Mothers of Invention, and the great Stanley Clarke. Duke wailed on the Fender Rhodes! He did this with his great sense of touch—using basic chord voicings in the left hand, accented by rhythmic licks and kicks in the right hand. To hear his masterful synth soloing, check out "Brazilian Love Affair." A great arranger, vocalist, songwriter, and trained jazz musician, Duke hit the charts in 1977 with "Reach for It," and a year later with "Dukey Stick." Listen to these tracks for classic keyboard lines and keyboard patches he helped popularize.

Prince

Prince is one of the few artists who has written, arranged, produced, and performed (both vocally and instrumentally) most of his own material. Prince took his rock and funk influences and smashed out the Minneapolis sound. Songs like "When Doves Cry" and "Controversy" set the stage for this new, sexy funk experience. With the talents of musician Jimmy Jam on keyboards and the famed group The Time, Prince helped bring live band concerts to the stage in a time when other groups were falling by the wayside to disco. Prince's sound borrowed many of Little Richard's and James Brown's successful attributes: a tight rhythm section, funky polyrhythmic drum patterns, poppin' bass lines, and "shackin'" rhythm guitar. But the biggest part of the sound was the keyboards. Prince used stabs and accents like Fred Wesley and the Horny Horn section, but now the keyboard played these parts. He also sustained diminished chords through the downbeat of the measure, resolving to the I chord on beat 2! Oh yes, and don't forget that this was all accompanied by crash cymbals and dance moves—very musical indeed. Prince's first hit single in 1980 was "I Wanna Be Your Lover." Listen to the keyboard progression of this song—a progression that has literally become a mainstay in pop music today. Its use of triads (though not always the 1st, 3rd, and 5th)—voice led in a rhythmic figure that sets up the groove even when isolated—demonstrates some of the basic ingredients needed to make funk. Prince produced The Time in the 1981 release *What Time Is It?*, including the recordings "777-9311," "Jungle Love," and "Cool."

Chapter 1 — Chord Progressions

The object of this first chapter is to get you visualizing chord voicings without the pressure of reading notes or figuring out complex rhythms. Following are some chord progressions found in many ballads and uptempo grooves. Voice leading is a must here! The chords are simple, but when used rhythmically, they become powerful expressions of musical statements. Remember: it's the cyclical use of these progressions that produce the groove factor. Although these chords may be played using just one hand (the right hand), they may also be played using both hands, thus allowing you to *comp* (a shorthand term for *accompany,* or back up) using voicings that don't interfere with the bass player. There are many times that the bass or low register of the keyboard is not needed—hence, both of your hands will be busy doing something! Play through each progression over and over until your fingers get used to making the transition from one chord to another. We'll apply these progressions to rhythmic phrases in Chapter 2.

Fig. 1—Use of minor 7th chords

○ Play these notes centered around middle 3 – C
● May be played down an octave

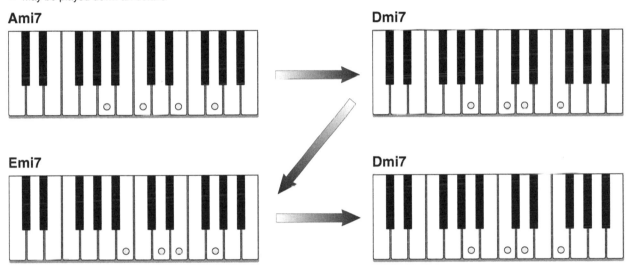

NOTE: Play all chords over root (in left hand), unless otherwise indicated.

Fig. 2—Use of major chords

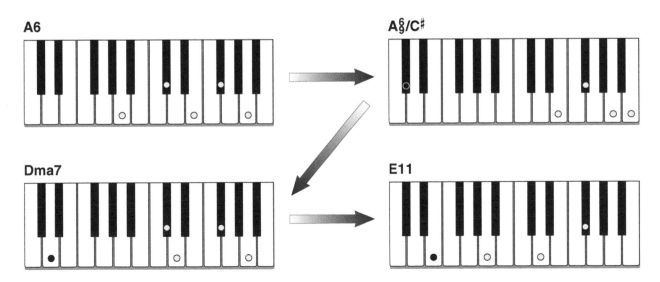

Fig. 3—Use of dominant chords

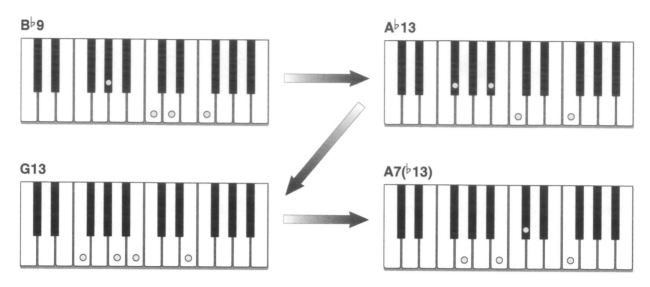

Fig. 4—Use of II-V

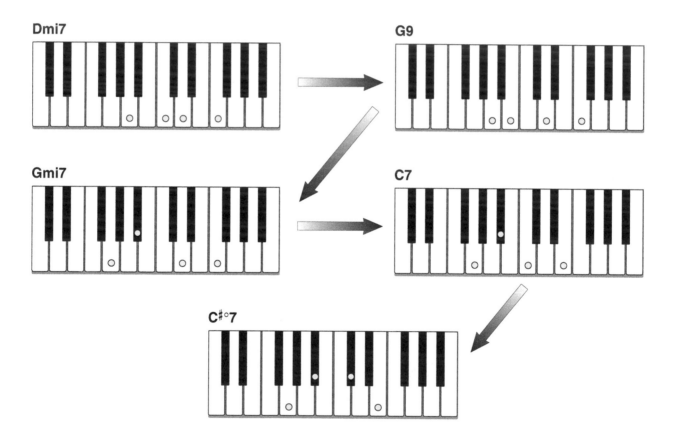

Fig. 5—Diatonic Cadence

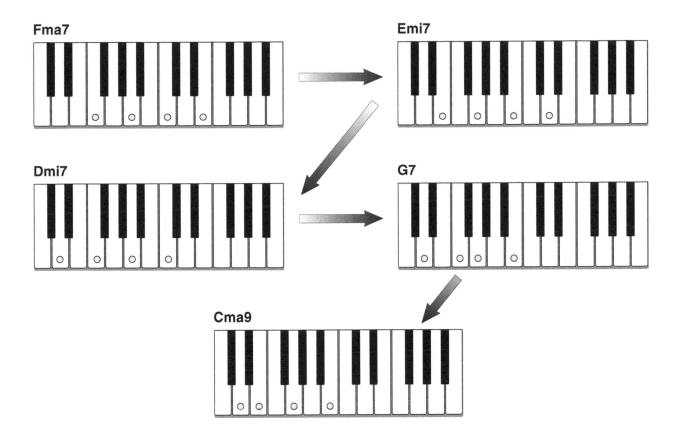

Fig. 6—Deceptive Resolution

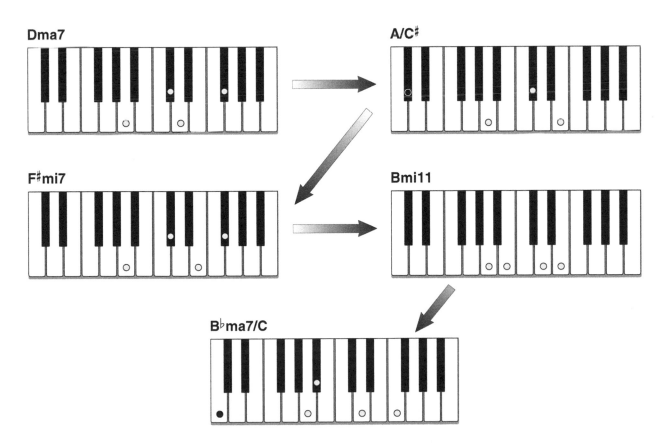

Fig. 7—Major I-IV-V

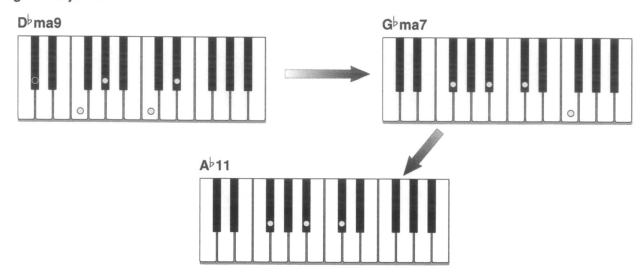

D♭ma9   **G♭ma7**

A♭11

Fig. 8—Minor I-IV-V

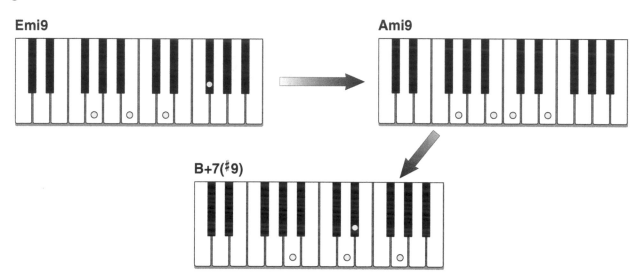

Emi9   **Ami9**

B+7(♯9)

Fig. 9—Major I-VI-II-V

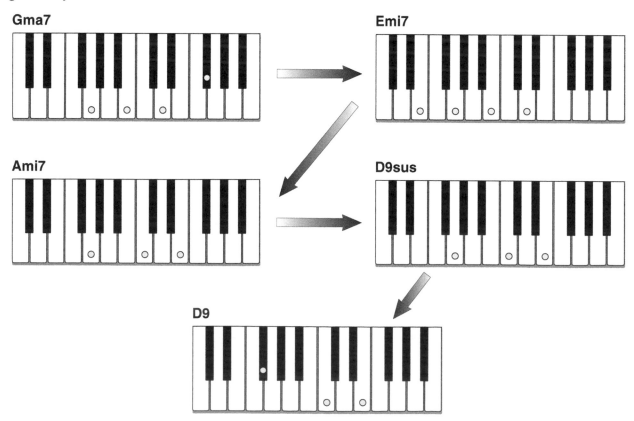

Gma7   **Emi7**

Ami7   **D9sus**

D9

Fig. 10—Minor I-VI-IV-V

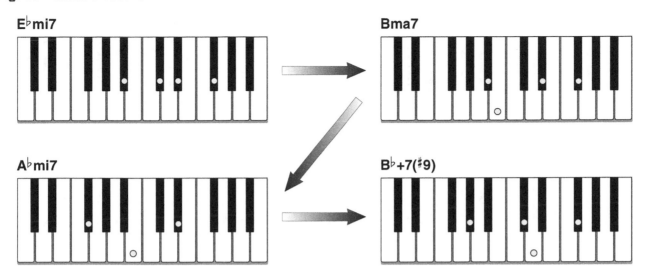

E♭mi7 → Bma7

A♭mi7 → B♭+7(♯9)

Fig. 11—Subdominant Chords

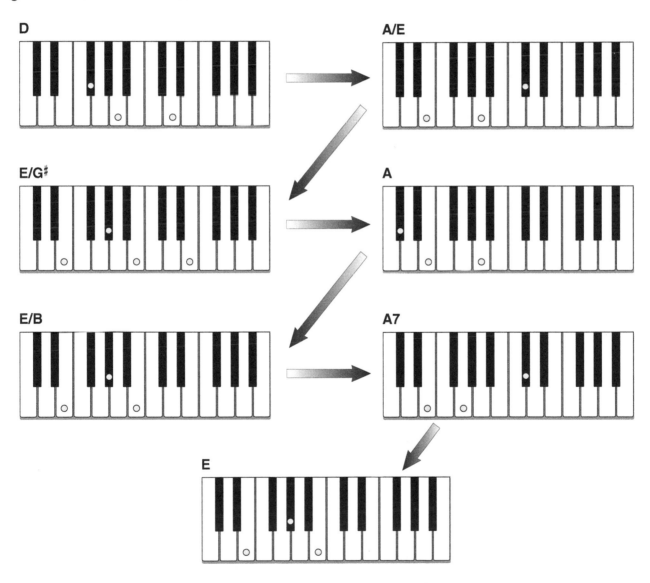

D → A/E

E/G♯ → A

E/B → A7

E

Fig. 12—Suspended Chords

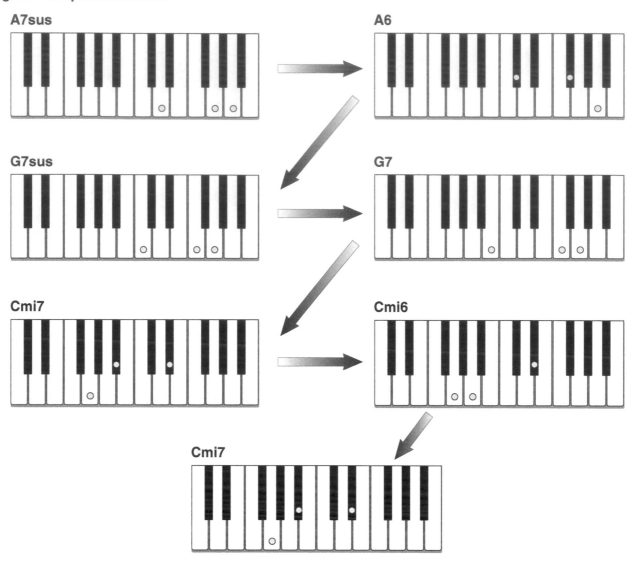

VOICINGS

Shortcuts to Chord Recognition

SHAPES: Chords are not that hard to find if you can make basic shapes out of the keyboard layout. Most triads, both major and minor, take the shape of a rounded "W."

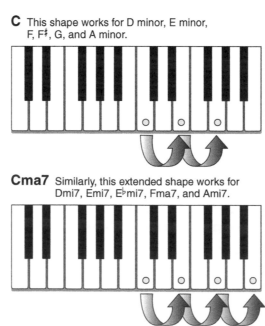

C This shape works for D minor, E minor, F, F♯, G, and A minor.

Cma7 Similarly, this extended shape works for Dmi7, Emi7, E♭mi7, Fma7, and Ami7.

G7 Again, using this shape will help you to find many chords. You can experiment with these shapes and create custom voicings of your own!

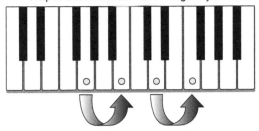

B♭ This pyramid shape works also for D, E, and A.

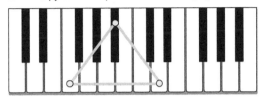

E♭ This upside-down pyramid makes another visual shape of chord possibilities. It also works for A♭, D♭, F♯ minor, G♯ minor, and C♯ minor.

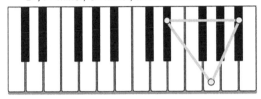

A♭ma7 Combining two triangle shapes can add extensions onto your triads.

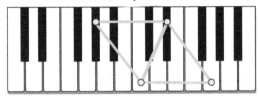

E13 This shape may also be used to layer other triads that share the same setup; i.e., a triad in the right hand, played over on E triad in the left forms Ama9.

C9 By combining and mixing the various shapes, endless possibilities emerge.

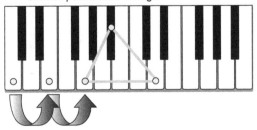

D7

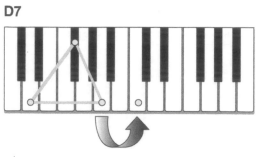

$B\flat°7$ Stretch your imagination and visualize; once you come up with something you like, find another starting point to create more.

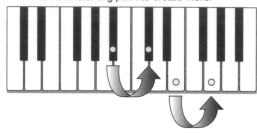

FORMULAS: Many chords use irregular-shaped forms, so other ways of finding them are needed. Below are some suggestions.

BASIC CHORD LAYOUT

- Major Chord: 1–3–5
- Minor Chord: 1–♭3–5
- Diminished Chord: 1–♭3–♭5–(♭♭7)
- Augmented Chord: 1–3–♯5
➠ Extensions (notes added to the basic chord to add color): 6, ma7, ♭7, 9, ♭9, ♯9, 11, ♯11, 13, ♭13

Major 7th Chords

1) Take the 3rd note of the major scale.
2) Form a minor triad
3) Place over tonic (root).
4) Emi/C=Cma7

Cma7

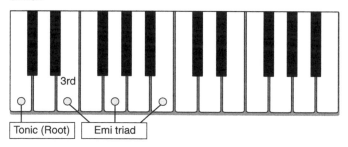

Major 9th Chords

1) Take any note (root).
2) Go to the 3rd interval of the scale.
3) Form a minor 7th chord.
4) Place over the root.
5) Emi7/C=Cma9

Cma9

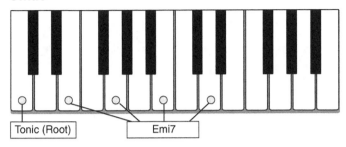

Major 11th Chords

1) Take any note (root).
2) Count down a whole step and form a triad.
3) Place the triad over the root.
4) C/D=D11

D11

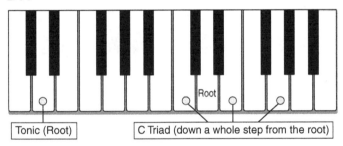

Minor 9th Chords

1) Take any note (root).
2) Go to the ♭3rd of the scale.
3) Form a major 7th chord from the ♭3rd.
4) Place the major 7th chord over the root.
5) Fma7/D=Dmi9

Dmi9

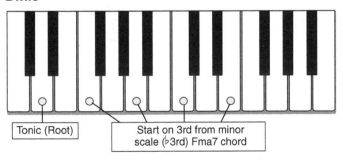

Minor 11th Chords

1) Take any note (root).
2) Go up a 4th.
3) Add a 4th.
4) Add another 4th.
5) Three stacked 4ths = minor 11th chord

Dmi11

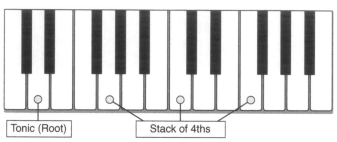

Major 11th Chords

1) Take the V7 chord.
2) Place over the tonic (root).
3) G7/C=Cma11

Cma11

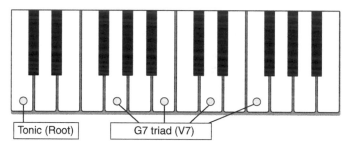

♯11th Chords

1) Take a triad.
2) Count down a whole step.
3) Play the triad over that note.
4) F/E♭=E♭13(♯11)

E♭13(♯11)

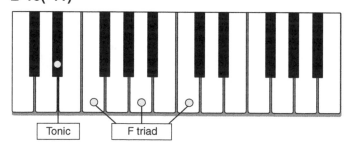

Dominant 7th(♭9) Chords

1) Take a note.
2) Form a diminished 7th chord.
3) Count up a whole step from the root of the diminished 7th chord.
4) Play the diminished 7th chord over that note.
5) C°7/D = D7(♭9)

D7(♭9)

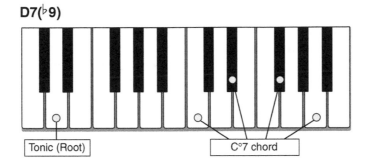

NUMERIC REPRESENTATION: Sometimes, seeing a voicing in a numeric setup helps to spell out a chord more quickly. The chords below are laid out from the bottom of the keyboard (at the bottom of each diagram) to the top.

Cma7
5/G
3/E
ma7/B
Root/C

G♭7(♭5)
♭5/C
9/A♭
♭7/E
Root/G♭

E7(♯9)
♯9/G
♭7/D
3/G♯
Root/E

Dmi7(♭5)
♭5/A♭
♭3/F
♭7/C
Root/D

Gmi6
6/E
♭3/B♭
Root/G

Ama7(sus2)
ma7/G♯
5/E
2/B
Root/A

C♯7(♭9)
♭9/D
♭7/B
3/F
Root/C♯

D♭7(♯9♭5)
♯9/E
♭7/C♭
♭5/G
3/F
Root/D♭

B♭13
13/G
3/D
9/C
♭7/A♭
Root/B♭

Dmi9
♭3/F
♭7/C
5/A
9/E
Root/D

B7(♭13♯9)
♭13/G
3/D♯
♯9/D
♭7/A
Root/B

A♭13(♯11)
13/F
♯11/D
9/B♭
Root/A♭

E♭ 6/9
9/F
6/C
3/G
Root/E♭

F♯°7
♭7/E♭
♭5/C
♭3/A
Root/F♯

G♯11
11/C♯
3/C
♭7/F♯
Root/G♯

Many times, when musicians begin writing a chart, chord labels can get confusing: "What do I name this chord? Is it a Gmi9 or B♭ma7?" While a certain amount of discerning can come from your ear, there are a few things to look for that will help you accurately identify a chord's function:

1) *Check the key signature first.* This will help you set up your tonal center, from which you can analyze your song's structure.

2) When in doubt, the quickest way is to *check the bass note.* This works when the bass line is not very busy and shows consistent patterns. It the bass line is busy, generally the first or last note of the figure will help identify the chord.

3) Listen carefully to try and identify if the chord has a *major* or a *minor* sounding tone quality. You may have decided on what group of notes (chord) to play first, and what you play thereafter may effect what you name a chord. Hence: where you're going and where you're coming from can make a difference.

For example, take a look at the following chord progression:

Gmi7	Ami7	B♭ma7	C
Minor	Minor	Major	Dominant

This same chord progression could be named:

B♭6	F/A	Gmi9	C/A
Major	Major	Minor	Minor

Another example to consider:

| B♭ | E♭ | E♭6 | F7 |

But since you've named the I-IV-?-V with B♭, E♭, and F7, the question mark that was labelled E♭6 would make more sense labelled as a II. After checking with the bass note (which is C), then the correct assumption is Cmi7 instead of E♭6.

| B♭ | E♭ | Cmi7 | F7 |

4) Try to identify chords by the *most common tones* belonging to one chord. Avoid long chord names and extensions. Most chords can be named using very basic names, e.g. Gmi7(♭13♯11)/E♭ could be easily named E♭9.

5) *Be careful about 7th chords.* Sometimes you may name a chord G♭7 when you actually intended it to be a G♭ma7! This latter chord is interpreted quite differently from the dominant-sounding G♭7. Always include ma7 or mi7 in the chord name if this is the chordal sound you want. Funk music utilizes ma7, mi7, and dominant 7 chords quite frequently throughout a song, so proper identification is important.

Chapter 2 Rhythms

The objective of the exercises in this chapter is to familiarize you with the various rhythm patterns you can utilize over a chord progression. Some examples of this are:

- *Pad*—to sustain a chord in whole notes

- *Anticipation*—to sustain the whole notes but anticipate the next measure by a sixteenth note

- *Color*—to add texture with glissandos or arpeggios in the upper register with the right hand as you pad with the left

- *Comp*—to play the chords with added rhythm phrases, using 3rds, 4ths, or 6ths

- *Syncopation*—very busy left and right hand movement

Following are some chord progressions using some of these techniques. First, we'll go through several rhythm patterns, then we'll apply the chord progressions from Chapter 1.

When playing these rhythms, keep in mind a steady eighth-note feel. Then try swinging the eighth-note groove in your head. Note: while the bass part may be swung, the drummer may play his part straight; or one of the guitar parts may swing while the other remains steady. It's this combination of feels that can make the groove funky.

For the following examples that include audio, listen or play along with the recorded keyboard part; the last time each figure is repeated, the keyboard on the recording drops out so you can practice by yourself with the drums.

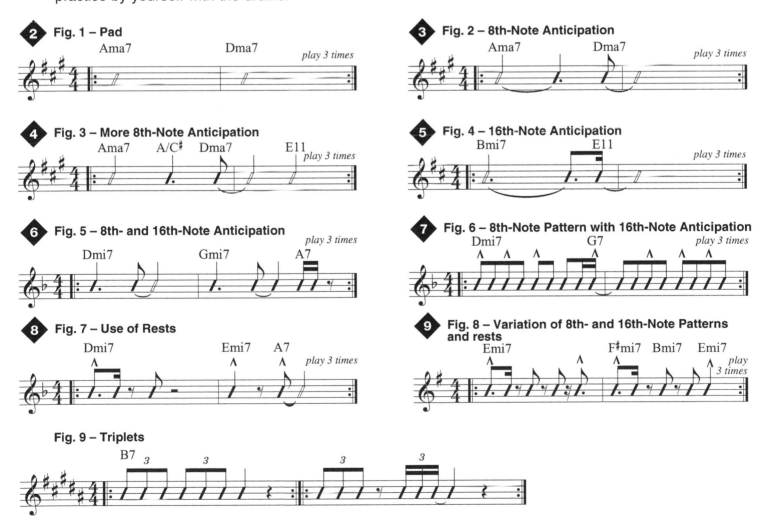

Fig. 1 – Pad

Fig. 2 – 8th-Note Anticipation

Fig. 3 – More 8th-Note Anticipation

Fig. 4 – 16th-Note Anticipation

Fig. 5 – 8th- and 16th-Note Anticipation

Fig. 6 – 8th-Note Pattern with 16th-Note Anticipation

Fig. 7 – Use of Rests

Fig. 8 – Variation of 8th- and 16th-Note Patterns and rests

Fig. 9 – Triplets

Slides

A *slide* is sometimes referred to as a *rake* or *gliss.* (short for *glissando*). It is used freely in funk music to "bring in" the song after the drummer counts off, or it is used to signify an upcoming change in the following measure. Most frequently, keyboard players use the bottom of their right-hand palm to slide up the keyboard and the nail of their right-hand thumb to slide down the keyboard; inversely, for the left hand, the bottom of the palm is used to slide down the keyboard while the thumbnail is used to slide up the keyboard.

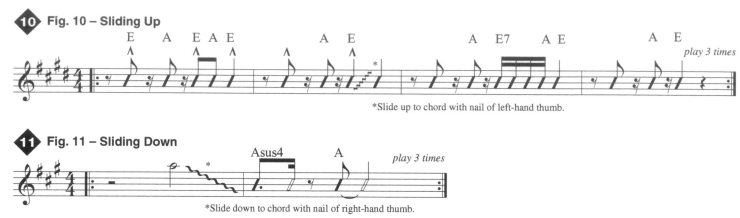

*Slide up to chord with nail of left-hand thumb.

*Slide down to chord with nail of right-hand thumb.

Playing to the Bass Rhythm

Another approach to playing keyboard rhythms is to play along with the rhythm of the bass line. Here are several examples:

Chord Progression Rhythms Using Voicings from Chapter 1

Now we'll use all those voicings we learned in Chapter 1 to create some great progressions.

Classic Funk Rhythms

There are many rhythms keyboard players used throughout the course of funk to place themselves in the pocket of the groove. As grooves altered over time, so did the rhythm of the chords. There are specific patterns that evolved out of the music, thus marking their place in time as classic patterns of each era. Below are a few examples.

Sounds of the '60s

Sounds of the '70s

Fig. 29

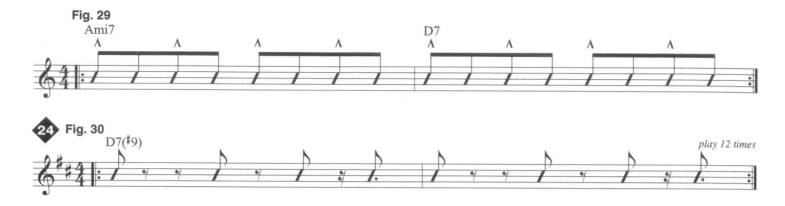

24 ▶ **Fig. 30**

play 12 times

Sounds of the '80s

Fig. 31

25 ▶ **Fig. 32**

play 12 times

Chapter **3** Two-Hand Rhythm Technique

For the funk keyboardist, two-hand rhythm technique is probably the most outstanding feature of this genre. While all music is played with both hands, it is the rhythmic patterning, or two-hand interplay, of funk that makes the music funky! Whether you're playing the Rhodes, the organ, or the clav, most of these rhythms are interchangeable, though some have become favorites to the particular instrument. For example, some licks most organists will undoubtedly use are grooves that Billy Preston or Chester Thompson have made signature in their music. The same is true for Herbie Hancock or Dexter Wansell and the Fender Rhodes. Clav kings like Herschel Happiness and Stevie Wonder have also made their mark. Two-hand technique can't be easily transcribed, so the following manuscripts are just a basic framework from which you may begin learning the technique. Practice them as written, and then try swinging the groove. The only way to get it is to play it over and over again. Have fun with them—they are great warm-down exercises (after you've done your usual routine). Play some of these rhythmic phrases along with the audio and with some of the suggested listening material (be sure to transpose to the key of the recording). Listen, listen, listen, since many times the keyboard parts are way back in the mix. Try to pick out the part clearly, either by putting the song through your mixer and adding EQ or by panning to one side or the other. Sometimes a part may be heard very clearly by listening from an adjacent room (so your ear is not right next to the speaker). This can be a great ear-training exercise.

Eighth-Note Patterns

The objective of Figs. 1-8 is to gain independence in the left and right hands. While one hand is rhythmically constant, the other hand fills in the rhythm—usually while the first hand is at rest. This exercise will also assist you in reading rhythms. Simply choose a single note (e.g., C in each hand), use your thumb or third finger, and practice reading the rhythms. Feel the alternating pulse, and try to keep good time. Play several times at a slow tempo, then speed up to a sixteenth-note feel.

Right Hand

Fig. 1

Fig. 2

Fig. 3

Fig. 4

Left Hand

Fig. 5

Fig. 6

Fig. 7

Fig. 8

Alternating Left and Right Hand Rhythms

Now let's use eighth-note patterns with single notes. Choose a Rhodes or clav sound, and place accents on the downbeats. Notice that the alternating note is the octave—a very common approach.

26 **Fig. 9**

play 5 times

Leading with the Left Hand

Add chords to the rhythm, playing the pattern slowly at first until you get the feel (without playing too "jerky"). Once you get it smooth, speed up the tempo.

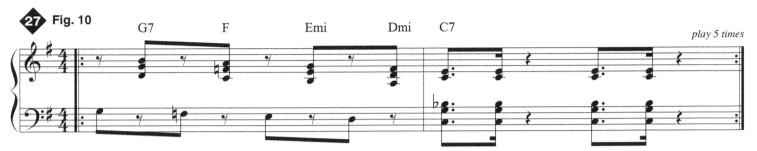

Leading with the Right Hand

This approach may feel awkward at first, but after several repetitions it will feel more natural. Again, alternating rhythms between the left and right hand is the goal.

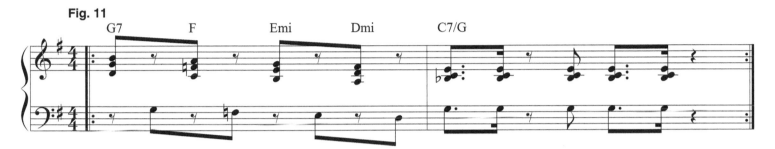

Now that we've played alternating octave/chord rhythm patterns, we can add the fifth of the scale to the left-hand pattern to provide a choice of notes.

Another way to play alternating rhythms is by playing chords with both hands, either by doubling the voicing in both hands or by filling out one chord between them, and then adding a rhythmic pattern.

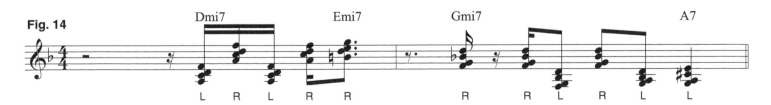

Adding sixteenth notes to the pattern boosts the excitement level. The quicker rhythms cause your adrenaline to surge, and, without thinking about it, your energy kicks into another level. These patterns are fun, but beware: at first the muscles in your shoulders and forearms may ache. This is called *chop-building!* Relax, pad a few bars, and then jump back into the groove. Be watchful of your timing—don't rush.

For Fig. 15, choose a clav sound. First, play the figure as written, and then replace the melody with chords.

Fig. 16 sets up a *call and response* between the left and right hands by adding another octave into the groove.

Sixteenth-Note Patterns

So far we've primarily used eighth-note patterns to get used to the feel and rhythmic placement of the left and right hands. The following exercises will help you in reading sixteenth-note patterns. Again, syncopation is the objective. Count aloud, playing one hand at a time, then combining the two. The mixture of eighth- and sixteenth-note rhythms, including rests, are the foundation of funk rhythm patterns.

Play these figures over any of the funk drum grooves on the accompanying audio. This will help you "hold down the groove." Try creating your own rhythms by adding 3rds, 4ths, and broken chords in the right hand.

Fig. 19 – Adding rests

Fig. 20 – Adding fills

(fill)

Fig. 21 – Reading tied rhythms

Fig. 22 – Crossing the bar line

Chopping

Clav players enjoyed the "level playing field" of three black keys—hence, many funk clav parts were written in E♭ minor. Repeat the following figure until you start to ache. Soon it will feel natural and you won't have to think about what you're doing (actually emulating the rhythmic feel of the guitar!). Visually, your hand will rock from left (L) to right (R).

31 Fig. 23 – Left-hand exercise

play 4 times

fingering: 5 1 1 5   5 1   5 1 1 5   5 1
visual: L R R L   L R   L R R L   L R

31 Fig. 24 – Right-hand exercise
(cont'd)

E♭mi7

play 4 times

Now play both the left- and right-hand exercises together. It's a little tricky, but once you get the hang of it, you'll find yourself groovin'! Set the tempo at 80 bpm, gradually increasing it as you master the exercise at each tempo. This exercise is really a sixteenth-note feel, so the goal is to play it twice as fast as it appears here!

31 (cont'd) **Fig. 25 – Right and left hands combined**

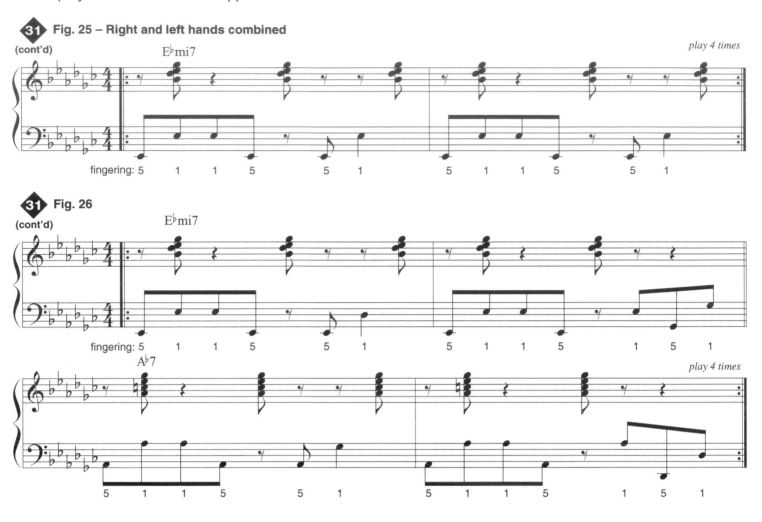

Fig. 27 is a variation of the same pattern. Try swinging the groove.

Let's finish off the chapter by combining the techniques we've learned into a complete song built out of several grooves.

32 Two-Hand Groove

Chapter **4** Licks

Licks, also called *riffs,* can be described as "snippets or bits of a line that are used in a repetitive fashion." Sometimes these licks or riffs are played in unison with other players. They make great intros, endings, or connecting lines between sections. Most often they are used as pieces within solos. Other times, they are used as solo lines to make up a short solo using two sounds at once (i.e., clav and bass part).

When soloing, funk musicians had to find a way to express themselves in a way that stood apart from the jazz idiom. They played "inside" the tonal center, however, many of their lines have their basis in bebop lines (without the constant key changes). Adding various rhythms to the funk groove gave them characteristics of their own. Repetition and the twisting of the same five or seven notes added energy. Always finding new ways to say something hip in a diatonic or one-chord setting was a challenge. The phrasing became most important because the solo had to be completed in a matter of four, eight, or sixteen measures. On the live gig or jam, the stretch could be extended. As funk music became more popular, the bands got bigger. In its heyday, the average band was at least ten pieces (drums, bass, lead guitar, rhythm guitar, keyboards, percussion, trumpet, sax, trombone, and lead vocals with the band singing backup vocals), all striving for a solo.

The objective of this chapter is to learn some of the lines that are used frequently in funk music to aid you in soloing. I've named chords that these lines work over; however, they may be interchanged. When listening to great soloists like George Duke or Bernie Worrell, check out their placement and phrasing. Also, don't limit yourself to the keyboardist; listen to other instruments, e.g. Fred Wesley (trombonist for James Brown).

Learning a lick is no good if you place it on the wrong pulse of the beat. Some of the most popular scales to use are the pentatonic and minor blues scales; the masters have cleverly made these very musical. After learning the licks, transpose them to other keys, adjusting your fingering to what feels natural and making the lines connect smoothly. Sometimes the orthodox way of playing a line makes it sound stiff. Experiment with different approaches: e.g,. hitting the strong downbeats with the middle finger will surely emphasize that tone.

33 Fig. 1 – Blues licks

34 Fig. 2 – Minor pentatonic licks

Many of these licks may be played over various chord types, such as dominant or altered chords; the chords posted are used as a key center from which you can hear where they may be placed harmonically. Make sure to transpose these licks through all keys.

36 Fig. 4 – Minor licks

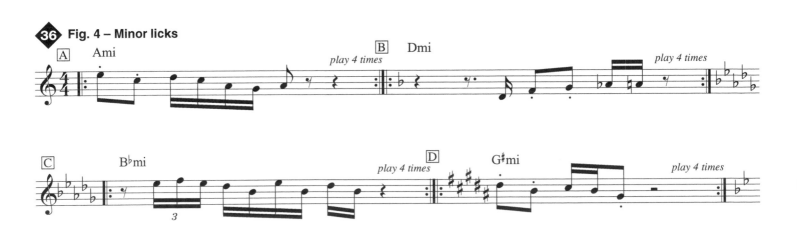

37 Fig. 5 – Fourth licks

38 Fig. 6 – Horn licks

Fig. 7 – Dominant 7th licks

Cadences

Cadences can be expressed as endings or beginnings of phrases. They are lead-ins or lines of release to end a section or bring in a verse. These lines are usually played by a lead instrument, like a keyboard or guitar; however, any instrument in the rhythm section can set up the cadence (even a drum roll or bass slide).

39 Fig. 8 – Cadences

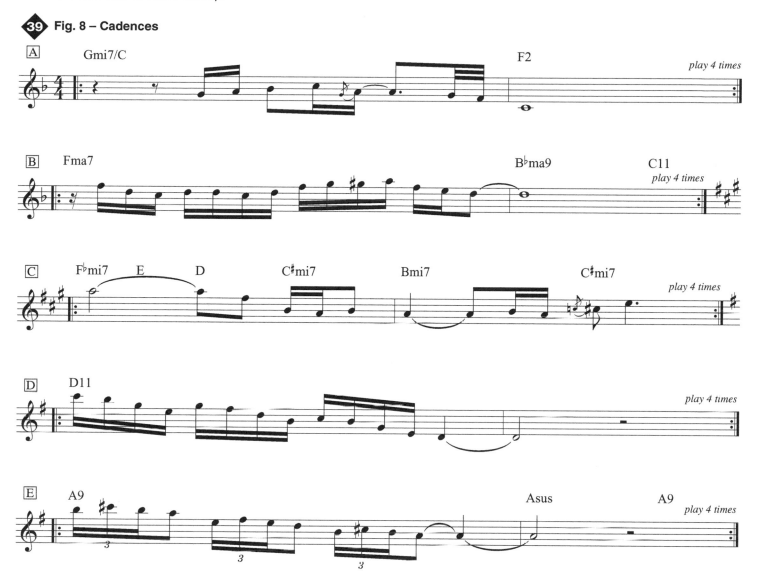

Chapter **5** The Pitch Wheel and Modulation

During the beginning of the funk era, keyboardists used only whatever effects were onboard their given instrument: the Fender Rhodes had tremolo or vibrato, the clav had some vibrato, and the Hammond B3 had its swell pedal to add dimension to its sound. Eventuallly, however, musicians started using gadgets like the Mutron phase shifter, Boss chorus, and even the wah-wah, to expand their arsenal. Until the advent of the synthesizer, keyboardists relied on these effects pedals (borrowed from guitarists) or utilized the reverb from the amplifier to add effects to their sound. One day, in the perpetual search for new sounds, the Arp synthesizer was invented, and keyboardists took this monophonic keyboard with great excitement. Thus was born the *pitch wheel,* which enabled keyboardists to emulate the bending effect already utilized by vocalists, guitarists, and horn players. *Modulation* was used to add vibrato to the tone. To date, there are three types of wheels:

1) *Round,* which rolls forward or backward to its maximum position, or sits neutral at home in the center. Two wheels are used: one for pitch, the other for modulation. Most players cup their left hand over the edge of the keyboard and use their left thumb to operate one wheel at a time (see Fig. 1A).

2) *Joystick,* which moves both left and right to the maximum bend positions. Holding the stick between the thumb and index finger and pushing forward creates modulation (see Fig. 1B).

3) *Ribbon,* a flat, touch-sensitive bar, made popular with the remote keyboards. Use either the pointer or middle finger to slide up or down, creating a pitch bend. Modulation is achieved by simply pressing harder on a given spot on the bar.

Some find more flexibility with the joystick and ribbon, but the round wheel is still the preferred choice for many.

Fig. 1 – Wheel types

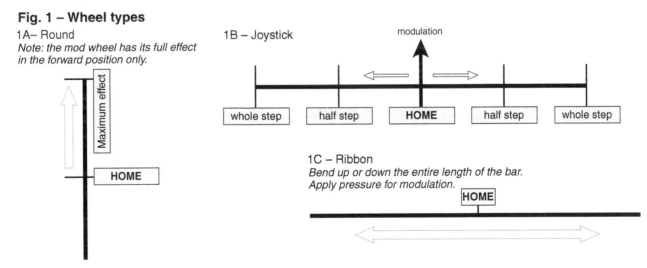

1A– Round
Note: the mod wheel has its full effect in the forward position only.

Maximum effect

HOME

1B – Joystick

modulation

whole step | half step | HOME | half step | whole step

1C – Ribbon
Bend up or down the entire length of the bar. Apply pressure for modulation.

HOME

Pitch Bending

Whole-Step Bends

Set pitch bend parameter to +2 (Achieving a whole step bend)

Bend (i.e. play C, hold it and move pitch wheel forward to its maximum position—D is sounded; or play C, hold it and move pitch wheel back to maximum position—B♭ is sounded.

Home (wheel in its neutral position)

Scoop (Bend before the note is pressed—first push wheel back to its maximum position and hold it there; press a key, i.e. C; while holding the note, bring wheel forward to home position, i.e. B♭ to C is sounded. This also works in reverse.)

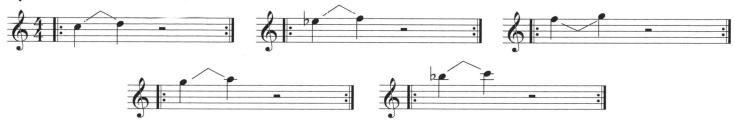

Half-Step Bends

After practicing the whole-step bend, now set your bend to +3, so that you can have the option of bending a half step or a whole step. You'll have to experiment to find the correct position of your pitch wheel for these intervals. Of course, the maximum position will result in a ♭3rd interval.

To achieve a half-step bend:

1) Play a note (i.e. C)

2) Play the note a half step up (i.e., C♯)

3) Noq, play C again and move the wheel until you hear C♯. (You may have to stop and play C♯ a few times until you get the pitch into your memory.)

To achieve a whole-step bend:

1) Play a note (i.e., C)

2) Play the note a whole step up (i.e., D)

3) Now play C again and move the wheel until you hear D. (Again, you may have to play D a few times until you get the pitch into your memory.)

40 Fig. 3 – Half-step bends

(cont'd)

Whole-Step Bend Exercises

Practice the following figures until you can match the way they sound on the audio.

40 Fig. 4

(cont'd) [A]

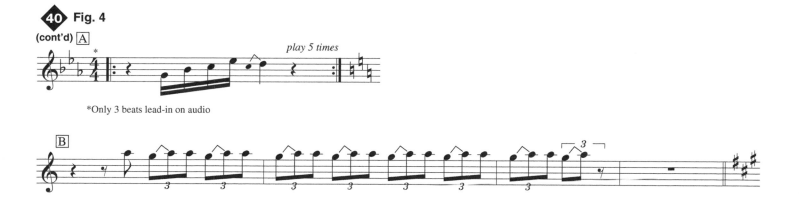

*Only 3 beats lead-in on audio

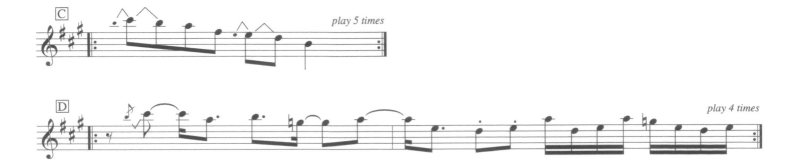

Half-Step Bend Exercises

Once you have the whole-step bend exercises mastered, move on to the following half-step bend exercises. Practice the figures until you can match the way they sound on the audio .

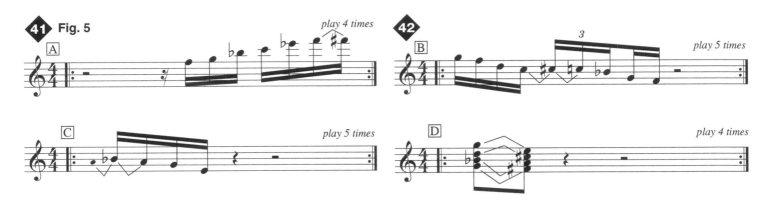

Modulation

The modulation wheel is a very effective tool in synth playing. Modulation is used to add vibrato to a sound, and most keyboards have pre-programmed modulation settings. In the old synths, you could set the speed and type of modulation (i.e., sawtooth, squarewave, or triangle). With the advent of midi, these signals are sent via midi. Depending on your keyboard, whether it be a wheel or joystick, move it to its maximum position forward to achieve the full effect.

Modulation Wheel Exercises

Play the following figures with the right hand and push back the modulation wheel with the left hand.

Fig. 6

Chapter **6** Synth Bass

One of the hottest sounds to emerge from the synthesizer is the synth bass—an instrument that is approached quite differently than the fretted bass guitar. Though it was only a monophonic synthesizer that introduced this sound, the Mini-moog reigned king for a long time and added a new dimension to the bass sound. Again, pitch bend and modulation were added features that further enhanced this sound. Playing the bass synth can be fun since it lends itself to a different creative expression than the typical two-hand piano technique. The fingering is somewhat unconventional, and uses the middle finger and thumb of both hands to hold down the groove. With the added versatility of a keyboard interface, key-bass players found new ways of "showing off." One memorable technique was an octave slide down into the downbeat. Another was a technique I've coined "the hop," where the bassist leaps into the upper register, plays a few notes ("grace notes" or "pickup notes"), then glides back down into the lower register just in time for the next downbeat. These notes are an integral part of bass synth technique and have become as much a part of the groove as the line itself.

Many bands used both the bass keyboard and bass guitar to thicken the sound. Before the invention of the five-string bass, bassists tuned their four-strings down to the lower E♭ or D. To get that deep sound, many synth bass songs were written in keys like E, E♭, or D. In the following examples, you'll find bass lines in some of these common keys.

Chapter **7** Multiple Keyboard Playing

Funk keyboard players would often have many keyboards in their setup, so playing polyrhythmic parts became part of the gig. This chapter focuses on grooves that utilize multiple keyboards. Generally, keyboardists play synth and Rhodes on the choruses, then switch up and play Rhodes and clav on the verses. Try switching hands as well; most keyboard players would set up their keys either to the left or right (so they'd be accessible to the hand that felt more comfortable playing each part). Independence is the key here. Double- and triple-tier keyboard stands have helped with this problem, but the better you are at playing any part with either hand, the better off you'll be in the long run. Undoubtedly, solos are taken with the right hand almost exclusively. Aside from this, other limitations crop up (e.g., the sounds in one synth are more appropriate for a part, quick patch changes, coordination with the sustain or volume pedal, or the use of pitch and modulation wheels). All of these parts are generally interchangeable. Experiment and enjoy!

51 Fig. 1

52 Fig. 2

53 Fig. 3

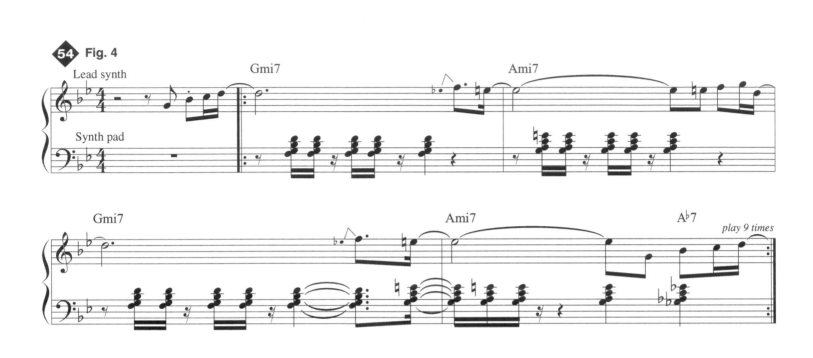

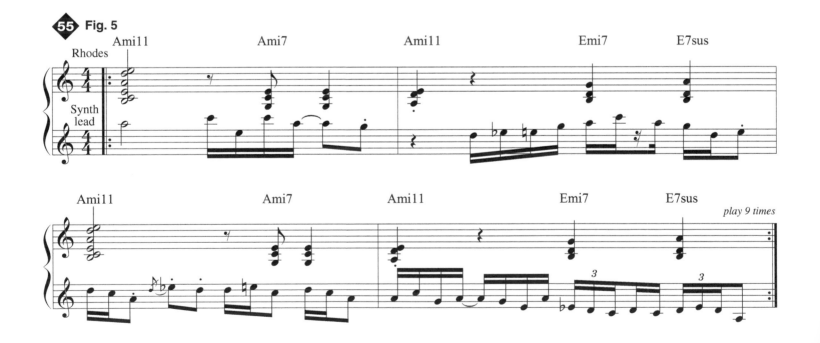

Chapter **8** Grooves

The most important part of funk music is the groove. After practicing voicings, chord progressions, and licks, the feel of the groove itself is what you should work on. The power of the groove lies in its ability to make people dance. This music is uptempo, driving, and energetic, and it should pulsate through the musician and lock into a single groove engine. This chapter focuses on various keyboard grooves that are found in many funk recordings. Start out by tapping the rhythms out before you begin to play. It helps to play both the left and right hands at once at a very slow tempo; because there are so many rests and dotted notes, it may be more difficult to read the parts separately. After you master them at a slow tempo, then swing the groove (eighth notes played as triplets), and play the whole part using different keyboard sounds. Repeat them many times and practice with a metronome—keyboard players are expected to keep good time! After hearing the audio examples and learning the parts correctly, *stop reading the groove*—just relax and feel it. The exercises are short and easy to commit to memory. Transpose them to other keys, and try writing your own grooves and making them a part of your style. Now that you're on your way to being a funk-master, remember: put it on the *one!*

56 Fig. 1 – Rhodes

57 Fig. 2 – Rhodes

*play 1st time only

58 Fig. 3 – Synth

59 Fig. 4 – Rhodes

Funk Songs

76 Spank-It

3 in '94

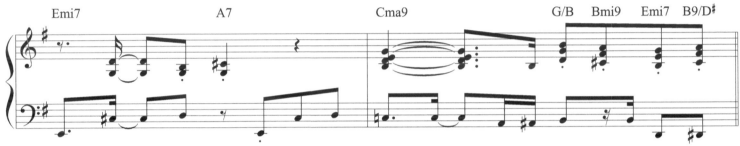

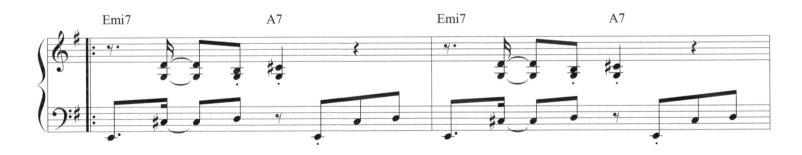

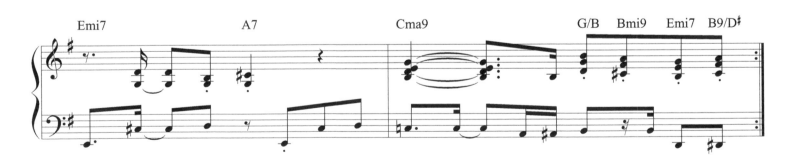

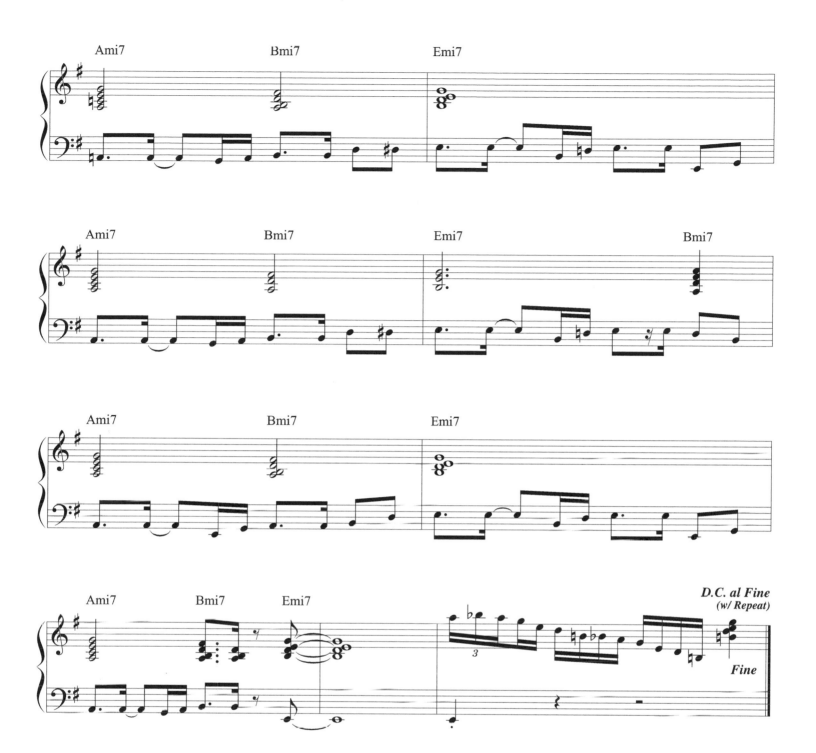

◆78 Lin-Lin

Donna

◈ Staffoly

◆ In Vain

About the Author

Born and raised in the city of Philadelphia, Gail Johnson began playing piano at age 10. Having received a music degree from the Berklee College of Music, Gail currently splits her time between her staff position at Musician's Institute, her music director position at Norman Brown/Warner Brothers Records, songwriting and producing, managing talented actresses, piano instruction, and occasional appearances on TV. She has played with Jermaine Jackson, Morris Day, Bobby Womack, Brandi Wells, Blue Magic, Vesta, Eugene Wilde, Eddie "ET" Towns, Norman Brown, Milli Vanilli, Howard Hewitt, Phillip Ingram/Sherri Payne, among others.